About the Book

One of the highlights of the 1976 Winter Olympics at Innsbruck, Austria, was the stunning performance of gold medal winner, Dorothy Hamill. Dorothy's career, from her first pair of skates to her present position as the foremost women's figure skater in the world, is detailed in this warm biography. Her determination, self-discipline, and dedication make an inspiring story. Dozens of photographs supplement the text.

Dorothy Hamill
Olympic Champion
by Elizabeth Van Steenwyk

photographs (except where noted) by
David Leonardi

Harvey House, Publishers
New York, New York

Copyright © 1976 Harvey House.

All rights reserved, including the right to reproduce
this book or portions thereof in any form.

Library of Congress Catalog Card Number 76-10046
Manufactured in the United States of America
ISBN 0-8178-5522-X

Harvey House, Publishers
20 Waterside Plaza, New York, New York 10010

Published in Canada by Fitzhenry & Whiteside, Ltd., Toronto

*The author
gratefully acknowledges
the assistance of
Sonya Dunfield,
David Leonardi,
Robert Paul, and
William Udell.*

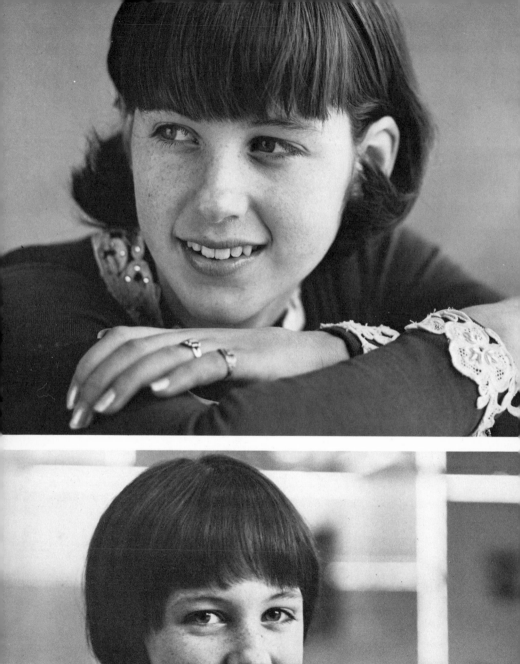

Chapter One

New snow sparkled under the winter sun as the young girls made their way to the ice-covered pond near their homes in Riverside, Connecticut. One of them, Dorothy Hamill, had received a pair of ice skates for Christmas and couldn't wait to put them on. Lacing up her boots with help from her friend's mother, Dorothy soon was ready. At first she could hardly stand and there were quite a few spills. Her ankles wobbled as she and her friends clung to one another for support. Dorothy laughed at her clumsiness and tried again and again. Her blue eyes sparkled and her cheeks grew pink in the cold air. Soon she was circling the pond with the other skaters.

After awhile Dorothy and her friends paused to rest and watch. Other beginners were on the ice finding their skating legs for the first time, too. There were some, however, who really knew how to skate. They could glide along on one foot, spin, and even skate backwards.

"That's neat," Dorothy said. "I want to learn how to do all that."

The eight year-old girl went home and asked her parents if she could take lessons. On Saturday morning Dorothy's mother drove her to the Playland Ice Rink in Rye, New York, and enrolled her in the beginners' class. It had started in November and this was now January. By the time class ended in March she was skating better than the rest.

This wasn't enough for Dorothy. She wanted to take more skating lessons. Before she could continue, however, her parents would have to buy her new skates. She had worn out the $6.95 pair they had given her for Christmas. Now with her new and better skates, everything else in life—school, swimming, and playing the violin—did not seem nearly as important.

During the summer Dorothy took studio group lessons. One day her teacher said, "I think you're ready to take the Preliminary test, Dorothy."

Dorothy looked quizzically at her. "What's a Preliminary test?"

Then her teacher explained. "The United States Figure Skating Association tests skaters to determine their progress. Do you have enough interest in skating to do this, Dorothy?"

The small, dark-haired girl smiled. Her eyes shone with excitement. She was interested all right. In fact she couldn't wait to take the test.

"What do I have to do?" Dorothy asked her teacher.

"Show that you are ready to learn to skate figures."

"What kind of figures?" Dorothy asked.

"All skating figures begin with a circle. Many of the circles are skated together so they look like the number eight on the ice. Sometimes you will skate three circles together instead of two. There are so many ways of skating these circles, or figures, that you will have to pass eight more tests before you have learned them all."

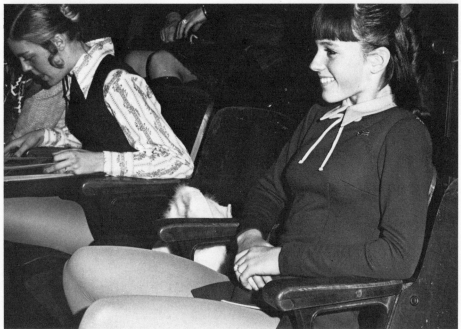

(Top) Working out in a studio. Practice makes perfect. (Bottom) Waiting for patch time. Hard to come by in those days.

In December, 1965, Dorothy passed her Preliminary and began her skating career. She was nine years old.

With private lessons Dorothy moved rapidly ahead. "Passing the USFSA tests is like passing grades in school," her teacher said. "After you have completed certain tests, you enter competitions at the regional or sectional levels to show what you can do."

Dorothy soon understood what her coach meant. After she had passed her First and Second tests, she competed in the North Atlantic regionals the following December as a Juvenile lady.

"They called me a lady even though I'm only ten years old," she told her parents. She soon learned that all girls, no matter what their age, are called ladies in competition. Dorothy liked the grown-up feeling it gave her.

Then she passed her Third test and could have competed as an Intermediate, the next step up. Instead Dorothy passed her Fourth test and jumped right to the next level, Novice division, skipping Intermediate class completely. She also joined the Rye (New York) Figure Skating Club and skated as one of their representatives.

As Dorothy's participation in figure skating grew, so did her need for practice or "patch" time. The rinks near Riverside were always crowded. Dorothy and her mother drove from New York to New Jersey or other towns in Connecticut, taking patch time at any hour of the day. Dorothy learned to eat, study, and even sleep in the car.

"Wake up, Dorothy," her mother said. "We're at the rink. How do you feel?"

Dorothy stretched and yawned. Then she said, "Great.

Early morning patch. Dorothy practices her school figures.

I feel great. Let's go, it's time for my patch."

One of the rinks at which she skated regularly was a forty-five minute drive from home. This rink was not even enclosed and it was here that she took her Fifth test in a strong wind with temperatures ten degrees below freezing.

Once in a while as she waited to practice or be tested, she felt left out and lonely. She knew she was missing activities that her friends enjoyed together. Later she would remember and say, "It was rough at time and I felt bad that I could never go to my friends' slumber parties. But I never skipped a lesson. Ice time was too hard to come by in those days."

Besides when Dorothy really thought about it, there was nothing else she'd rather do than skate.

Chapter Two

One day Dorothy was invited to visit the Skating Club of New York City. There she met Sonya Klopfer Dunfield, a vivacious young professional skater, who was Ladies' National Figure Skating Champion in 1951 and captain of the 1952 U.S. Winter Olympics team. Dorothy and Sonya liked each other right away. Soon it was agreed that Sonya would become Dorothy's coach, so Dorothy moved into New York City and stayed with family friends. She enrolled in public school and began daily three-hour lessons with Sonya.

Her coach soon discovered that the compulsory school figures were not Dorothy's favorite part of skating. To make them more interesting for the twelve year-old, Sonya appealed to Dorothy's well-developed sense of neatness and style.

"Take pride in your patch, Dorothy," Sonya said. "You want to trace that figure neatly so your neighbor on the next patch will admire you for it. If you're neat, you'll show good form. Good form, you know, is good style."

At Christmastime, Dorothy was invited to take part in the Winter Festival at Lake Placid, New York. She was one of the youngest and most exciting skaters performing there, and she received an enthusiastic response from the audience. Photographer David Leonardi was there that night and knew that he was watching a champion in the making. "One day she's going to be a National champion, for sure," he told Dorothy's father. "Just like Peggy Fleming."

From the movies he took that night, David made a flip book for Dorothy which she could study and use to improve her spins and jumps. Later in January David took more movies of Dorothy as she skated in the Eastern Sectional championships in Wilmington, Delaware. She didn't score too well in the figures, but her free style program carried her to third place. Dorothy became eligible to skate at the National level in Novice division.

In February of 1969, Dorothy flew to Seattle, Washington, for the Nationals competition. Only Sonya Dunfield went with her. On their first morning there, Sonya went into Dorothy's room to awaken her. She wondered if she'd find a frightened, homesick little girl. Instead Dorothy sat calmly watching television and trying on earrings from the little collection she always carried with her.

Later that day Sonya and Dorothy had lunch atop the famous Seattle landmark, the Needle. Dorothy also found time to send David Leonardi a postcard. She thanked him for photographs he had sent and added that she wanted to skate well. Her word for the weather was "terrible." In the afternoon Dorothy had a brilliant free skate practice.

"You almost jumped as high as Misha this afternoon," Sonya told her on the way back to their hotel.

"I'm going to jump higher than Misha tonight in my performance," Dorothy said, smiling.

Dorothy knew, of course, that she could not jump as

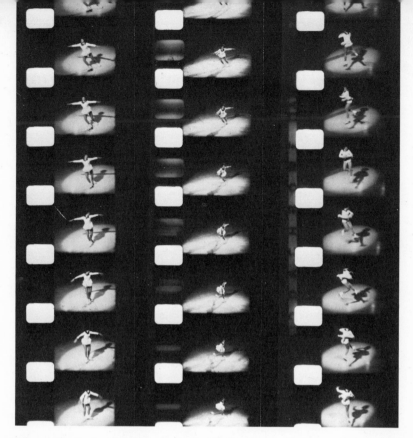

Film strips from David Leonardi's flip book.

high as tall, powerful John Misha Petkevich, the National Senior Men's skater. But she knew that she could try as hard as anyone else to skate her very best. And she did. Her strong performance was the winning one, too. At the age of twelve, Dorothy Hamill claimed the attention of the American skating world by becoming the National Novice champion.

The following season she entered competition at the Junior Ladies level and went to Buffalo, New York, to compete in regionals. In third place after the compulsory

*Dorothy's style and grace were evident in early competitive perform-
ances.*

school figures were traced, she eagerly looked forward to the evening's part of the competition. Free style skating was her favorite part of any performance. She could put all her spins and jumps together in a program set to music that she loved. One more practice session, she decided, and she'd be ready.

Finding the ice available for practice was difficult, but Dorothy's Dad managed to find a rink across the river in Erie, Ontario. It was early in the morning and the rink was freezing, but Dorothy felt lucky to get the extra practice. She pulled her fur hat down over her ears, adjusted her mittens, and stroked quickly out onto the dimly-lit ice. Before she knew what happened, she'd hit a rope stretched across the rink. The rope caught her, threw her backwards and out of control. She hit her head hard. She came off the ice dazed and bleeding. When her parents found a doctor to examine her, he would not let her compete that evening.

"You've had a concussion," he said.

Dorothy was heartbroken as she and her parents drove home.

"The judges agreed that you deserved to be passed on to the next competition," her Dad said. "Don't worry, Dorothy."

"But it feels like I lost," Dorothy said.

"You didn't lose," he replied. "You just weren't able to finish this time."

"No, Dad," Dorothy insisted. "I lost. Only one person wins. Everyone else loses."

And right then Dorothy made up her mind which person she wanted to be.

Practicing during Christmas vacation, 1970, at Lake Placid, New York.

Chapter Three

After a summer session of skating in Toronto, Dorothy returned to Lake Placid in September for lessons with the brilliant coach, Gustave Lussi. He recognized her strength right away and encouraged her to try for higher jumps and more speed. At the same time, he insisted she work for more controlled action. Dorothy loved his athletic approach to figure skating and her happy feelings were reflected in her warm, sunny smile. She learned to spot her spins and rarely traveled during one of them. Her attitude moves reflected a developing grace that showed she was beginning to understand and interpret her music.

Shortly before the series of lessons ended, Mr. Lussi discussed an idea for a new combination that he'd been thinking about. "Basically it's a flying camel layover, Dorothy," he said.

She followed his instructions, but couldn't seem to get it exactly the way he described it. Before she left Lake Placid, Dorothy tried several more variations and finally settled on one.

In New York she showed Sonya what she had been practicing. First she stroked into a flying camel layover. Then she bent her skating knee and dropped down into a sit spin.

"I like it," Sonya said. They worked together refining it.

Christmas Show at Lake Placid, 1970.

Then they put it in her program for the coming competition season.

The Eastern Sectionals were held at the Wissahickon Skating Club rink in Philadelphia, in January, 1970. David Leonardi gave Dorothy a pin from Davos, Switzerland, to wear for luck. Dorothy wore it with her other good-luck pin, a gold four-leaf clover given to her by the Rye Figure Skating Club.

Just before she skated her free style program, Dorothy became nervous and fought her usual case of stomach butterflies.

"Just remember," Sonya said, "what you're feeling is not nerves. It's really energy."

Dorothy calmed down and went out to skate a strong, consistent program. She became the Eastern Junior Ladies champion.

On Sunday afternoon following the competition, the winners were asked to skate in an exhibition.

"I'll do my competition number," Dorothy said. She was excited and happy that she'd been asked to skate again.

"But you don't have to repeat such a difficult performance," Sonya said.

"And you don't need to take the risks involved in your competition program," her Dad reminded her. "Just skate your exhibition number."

Dorothy wasn't convinced, but she finally gave in. National competition in Tulsa was just a couple of weeks away and she couldn't risk injury. But she didn't give a 'breather' or 'put-down' performance in Philadelphia that afternoon. With her enthusiasm for skating, she could never do less than her total best.

At the Nationals in February, Dorothy's first triumph came when she won the left change loop in school figures competition.

"Wow," she told Sonya. "I won a school figure. I really won."

The following day Dorothy skated to the center of the ice in a shocking pink costume. It was time for her free style program. After the music began she moved into the first double Axel she had ever attempted in a public performance. Her form was excellent and she landed it cleanly. Smiling, she continued the rest of her program, displaying footwork that was expert and fast. Her spins looked easy and were in exact positioning. Finally, just before the end of her three-and-a-half-minute program, she displayed the combination flying camel layover and sit spin. The audience rewarded her with a long, generous ovation and Dorothy responded with a smile that was warm enough to melt the ice.

After everyone had skated, Dorothy learned that she had won second place overall in National Juniors competition. Asked what she called the last combination in her program, Dorothy was stumped for an answer.

"It's just a variation on a camel," she said.

No one knows who first named it the Hamill camel, but the newspapers picked up the name and published it immediately. Soon skaters everywhere were practicing Dorothy's and Mr. Lussi's invention. Not many skaters ever had a move named for them. Thirteen year-old Dorothy felt thrilled to think it had already happened to her.

Chapter Four

After Nationals Dorothy went to work on her Eighth or "gold" test. With Sonya at her side, she practiced the paragraph double threes, loops, and brackets over and over again.

Both young women were anxious for the test to be completed, but for different reasons. Dorothy wanted to pass the last USFSA test and become eligible to skate in competition as a Senior lady. Sonya was expecting a baby, but wanted to see Dorothy through her last and hardest exam. Sometimes they wondered which would come first, baby or test time. Sonya's baby was born on May 27, 1970, and a few weeks later, on June 18, Dorothy wrote to David Leonardi to report that she had passed her Eighth test, noting that it required lots of work. She told him her plans to study skating in Toronto during July and August with time out for an appearance in a skating show at Lake Placid.

This year when Dorothy and Sonya went to Toronto for the summer session, they were joined by Sonya's month old son.

In January Dorothy returned to Lake Placid once again for the Eastern sectionals, thrilled to be skating as a Senior lady at last. Just before the free style competition, Dorothy skated out for her warm-up. Suddenly she found she

couldn't do anything. She couldn't land her Axels, her spins traveled, nothing worked. Sonya called her off the ice.

"What's wrong?" Dorothy asked, near tears.

"It's the ice," Sonya said. "It's hard, very slick, and much faster than what you're used to."

"But what can I do?" Dorothy said.

"Your timing is for different ice," Sonya said. "We can't change that, but we can change something else."

Quickly she told Dorothy to lace her boots in a different way. This changed her body balance, giving her the advantage of using her blades in a faster take-off. But there was no time to practice. Dorothy's scheduled warm-up time was over. She'd have to make her program work, depending on her talent and training to carry her through. When her name was called, she skated out to the center of the ice.

Then, with courage and determination, she gave a perfect performance and became the Eastern Sectional bronze medallist. She was eligible to skate at the National Senior level at last.

A blizzard greeted Dorothy and her parents when they arrived in Buffalo, New York, for the 1971 Nationals. In a card sent to David Leonardi, Dorothy called the weather awful, and her mother described the fifty-mile-an-hour winds as unbelievable.

But the weather didn't upset Dorothy's performance. In a dress described as a lucky red wool with snazzy trim, Dorothy skated to music from *The Firebird* and won fifth place in the National standings.

Late on Saturday night, after the competition had been completed, the Association officials asked to see Dorothy and her parents.

"We'd like to ask Dorothy to go to the pre-Olympic invitational in Sapporo, Japan," one of the men said. "Can she be ready to leave next Wednesday?"

Dorothy and her parents were excited and thrilled. At age fourteen, Dorothy became one of the youngest ladies ever to represent the United States in international figure skating competition.

On Sunday Dorothy drove home with her parents, spent Monday and Tuesday in a whirlwind of activity arranging tickets, visas, and clothes. She and Sonya also managed some final instructions and polishing sessions before Wednesday morning when Dorothy and her mother left for Japan.

At Sapporo, where the Olympics would be held the following year, Dorothy met Carlo Fassi, who gave her last-minute coaching instructions. Then Dorothy skated to third place in her first international competition. In spite of her busy schedule, Dorothy found time to shop for mementos for her friends at home. She sent David Leonardi a pin to add to his collection.

Later in the spring Dorothy wrote to him that she was going to Tulsa, Oklahoma, for the summer. She would be taking lessons from Carlo Fassi and his wife, Christa.

Dorothy had begun the next part of her skating career.

(Top, and bottom, left) Performance maneuvers including flying sit-spin during Dorothy's 4-minute program at the 1972 Eastern Senior Ladies competition at Hershey, Penna., held in December, 1971. (Below, right) Dorothy receiving championship trophy from Judge Ben Wright, 1972 Easterns.

Chapter Five

Dorothy came in fourth in the National Senior ladies' competition in 1972. She did not make the Olympic team, but felt proud and happy for her teammates who flew on to Sapporo.

On the day of opening ceremonies, Dorothy and her friends crowded around the television set to watch.

"Just wait," someone whispered to her. "Four years from now, you'll be marching with the U.S. team like that."

Dorothy smiled and wondered. She'd always dreamed of competing in the Olympics. Maybe one day it really would happen.

When Julie Lynn Holmes announced her retirement from amateur competition after the Olympics, Dorothy moved up to take her position on the World team. She joined the rest of her skating friends in Calgary, Alberta, Canada, and promptly wrote David Leonardi a postcard. She described the seventeen-below weather, the friendly people, and the lovely hotel. Dorothy told him her skating schedule and seemed pleased by the generous amount of patch time provided everyone. The fashion-conscious youngster also noted and commented on the Russians in their nice fur coats.

After winning seventh place in her first World's competition, Dorothy participated in several other international events later that year. In the summer she won the International Grand Prix championship at St. Gervais, France, and also carried home the Nebelhorn Trophy after placing first at Obersdorf, West Germany.

Dorothy's constant companions during her travels were her mother and her growing family of good-luck stuffed animals. The sixteen year-old girl missed her father as well as her older brother, Sandy, and her sister, Marcia, but she loved to go to new places and meet new people. European audiences knew figure skating and they cheered her appearances. The foreign skaters were friendly and helped Dorothy and her mother feel at home wherever they went. A skating life offered certain advantages, Dorothy found, in spite of all the hard work.

When she returned home, it was decided that she would continue her studies with Carlo Fassi. By now his new rink had been completed in Denver, Colorado. Once again Dorothy said goodbye to her family and moved out to the mile-high city.

"I don't like being away from home," Dorothy told a reporter. "But if I want to be a skater, that's the way it's got to be. My coach lives in Denver and I have to be there, too."

Dorothy enrolled in the upper school of Colorado Academy in nearby Englewood to continue her high school education. Her classes were arranged in a special block as they were for other skaters who attended there. Five

Dorothy with a couple of her good-luck stuffed animals. (Courtesy Broadmoor Hotel.)

classes in solid subjects were scheduled for Dorothy in the morning. Then she had the afternoon free for skating.

Mr. Dorais, her biology teacher, noticed that she immediately became popular with the other students. They liked her, not because she was a top skater, but for her friendly, thoughtful manner. Dorothy somehow managed to find time to attend school plays and games and date once in awhile. But it was hard. Figures and free style lessons with Carlo and ballet and physical training sessions crowded her full days.

The 1973 skating season introduced a new event in USFSA competition. It was called the compulsory short program. In it each contestant skated the same set of figures and combinations. The skaters called them elements. Dorothy won this part of the program over the National Senior ladies' champion, Janet Lynn. Dorothy showed excellent serpentine stepwork and a lingering, delayed Axel.

On free style night, Dorothy skated right after Janet. "That's a tough act to follow," she told her parents.

Then Dorothy skated out on the ice in a fire-engine-red chiffon dress. She stroked into her opening moves, making her jumps high and her spins faultless. Skating perfectly with her music, she skimmed over the ice, gliding from one move into the next. Like a dancer with perfect control, Dorothy never showed preparation for a move. She simply did it as if it were the easiest thing in the world. Ending her program with the Hamill camel, Dorothy received a standing ovation and became the National senior ladies silver medalist. Her smile was as bright as a shaft of sunlight when she came off the ice.

Chapter Six

Bob Paul, a gold medal winner in the 1960 Olympics, became Dorothy's choreographer. He helped set her skating to music in a rhythmic, appealing way. Bob discovered that Dorothy had amazing physical power for her five-foot, three-inch size. He already knew that the strength of her bubbling personality carried to the top row of any stadium.

Dorothy always rehearsed with Bob in a friendly, outgoing fashion. She listened closely to his directions and quickly understood them. Sometimes she liked to imitate other skaters she had seen and these sessions always ended in laughter.

Before her 1973 World's performance in Bratislava, Czechoslovakia, Dorothy experienced a case of nerves.

"Try not to think of this performance as anything special," Bob told her. "Do your program as if it were a regular, every-day practice."

Bob's advice helped Dorothy skate to fourth place in World competition. Later she spent many weeks on tour with other World skaters. She gave many other performances in the United States, helping to raise money for the USFSA Memorial Fund. Dorothy also entered another competition and won the Richmond International Trophy in England.

Dorothy's final 4-minute program at the 1974 Nationals held in February in Providence, R.I.

Then she returned to Denver once again to resume training for the 1974 Nationals. Janet Lynn had signed a contract with the Ice Follies now, so the Senior ladies title was vacant. Would it become hers? Dorothy wondered.

The 1974 Nationals competition began on February 6 in the civic center of Providence, Rhode Island. The arena seated ten thousand people and a glass-enclosed restaurant overlooked the blue-tinted rink. It was one of the largest and most beautiful buildings Dorothy had competed in.

Her first two compulsory figures were good, but the third looked shaky. She determined to do better in the compulsory short program. When her turn came, Dorothy leaped into her program, using music from Stravinsky's *Firebird* again. Her speed and ability dazzled the large audience. When she was finished they pounded their approval on the metal rails and seats.

The following evening the temperature had dropped to eighteen degrees outside. Inside the arena the atmosphere was warm with excitement and anticipation. Sold out for two days now, the arena was packed to the rafters. Tenley Albright, 1956 gold medal Olympics winner, was there and so was Janet Lynn. Dorothy's family and friends were scattered through the stadium waiting tensely for her performance.

Dorothy paced the dressing room and the halls in her shocking pink dress. She touched the gold four-leaf clover pin on her shoulder. Carlo whispered last minute instructions. Then her name was announced and she skated to the center of the ice.

With her music she stroked into her opening moves. Her

jumps were high and her landings light. "Don't forget to point your toe," she reminded herself. "Watch out for this loop coming next. Get it right. You've only got two minutes left, don't blow it now."

Then she whirled into her final moves and laced them together with intricate footwork. After a last spin, the National senior ladies title became hers at last.

Photographers came out to take her picture on the winner's platform. Among them was her friend, David Leonardi.

"You did it, Dorothy, you did it," he said. "Good luck at World's." Then he snapped his camera, capturing her brightest smile.

L to R: Charles Foster, Benjamin Wright, Kathy Malmberg, Dorothy, Julie McKinstry, Claire Ferguson, Ritter Shumway.

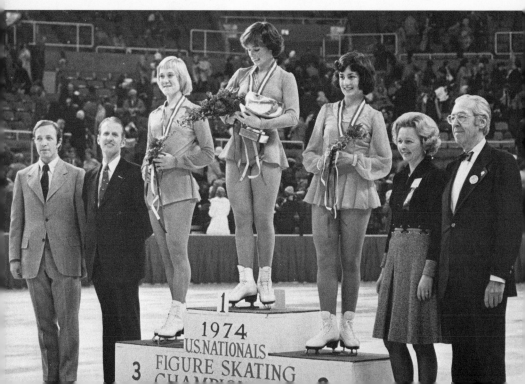

One month later Dorothy looked longingly at the city of Munich from a bus window. There would be no time to enjoy the attractions of the beautiful old city now. World competition began in Olympic Park soon. Later perhaps she would go to the Marienplatz and shop for gifts for her friends. Maybe she'd add some earrings to her collection.

Now it was Thursday and she had to concentrate on the compulsory figures which were a rocker, a change loop, and a paragraph double three. Dorothy led off the second figure and her tracing was good. In the short program she skidded a bit on her fast turns and landed off-balance in a jump. But she held on to second place behind Christine Errath of East Germany.

On Saturday night the final free skating event began. Dorothy waited until Gerti Schanderl of Munich finished her performance. Then she skated to the center of the rink. Suddenly the audience began to whistle and jeer. Dorothy looked up. Were they booing her? She skated off the ice to stand by her coach.

"That's not meant for you," Carlo said. "The audience is unhappy at the judges because they don't like the marks given to Gerti."

Dorothy returned to the ice, but the audience continued to be unruly. Finally she couldn't stand it any more, burst into tears, and skated off again. Moments later the audience calmed down. An official approached Dorothy. "Do you want to rest?" he asked.

"No way," she said, and returned to the ice for the third time.

Her music began and she determined to give the best

performance of her life. She lifted the opening Axel lightly, then flew into two Walleys. Her soaring double Lutz came next and she completed the entire four-minute program without a flaw. She received a perfect 6.0 from one judge and 5.9's from the rest.

Her smile sparkled from the winner's platform as she accepted the silver medal for second place. Dorothy had turned an unsettling experience into a winning event.

Dorothy skating in exhibition tours, Spring, 1974.

Chapter Seven

Dorothy graduated from Colorado Academy in June. Now she had even more time to devote to skating. She was on the ice from 7:15 to 9:30 every morning. Then she walked the short distance to the apartment where she lived with her mother. After breakfast Dorothy hurried to the physical fitness trainer. There she worked for two hours on running and resistance exercises. Back at the rink, she skated from 2:00 until 3:15 and then from 5:15 until 7:45. Once in a while Dorothy had time for dates with a boyfriend. She always had to be home by nine o'clock, however, so that she could get plenty of rest for the next day's practice.

A couple of months before the 1975 Nationals, Dorothy was scheduled to appear in Superskates in Madison Square Garden. The program would benefit the United States Olympic fund and she was eager to help. Just before she flew to New York, Dorothy had a practice session with Carlo.

"One more double Axel and then I've got to leave," Dorothy called to her coach. Somehow she misjudged her landing and fell. She limped off the ice and sat down.

"What's the matter?" Carlo asked.

"My knee hurts," she said.

"Skate around a few times so you don't stiffen up on

(Top) Relaxing on the lawn before the Olympic Tribute Show, November, 1975. (Bottom) L to R: Dorothy's father, Chalmers Hamill, Dorothy, and Mr. and Mrs. Marshall Baker, Wilmington, Delaware.

the plane," he advised.

Dorothy tried but now her foot hurt worse than her knee. Carlo said she'd better quit. She hurried back to the apartment to pack and just made the plane for New York. When she arrived her foot hurt so badly she couldn't put her shoe on. Dorothy's father took her to a doctor who taped her foot so that she could appear in Superskates. It upset Dorothy, however, that she couldn't skate her best and had to leave out most of her jumps.

After Thanksgiving Dorothy's foot was put in a cast and she wasn't allowed to skate until New Year's. With Nationals less than a month away, Carlo told Dorothy she could miss the competition if she didn't feel up to it.

"You can go directly to World's without skating at Nationals," he said. "You placed in the top five last year, so you are automatically eligible."

But Dorothy said no. She wanted to compete at Nationals in Oakland. After all she was the champion and had a title to defend.

Dorothy did not skate to full potential, but won her second National Senior ladies title anyway. Then she went on to Colorado Springs to participate in the 1975 World championships at the Broadmoor Hotel Arena.

She got off to a slow start, ranking fifth after a tight race in the figures. In the short program Dorothy fell from a flying sit spin. Then with an exciting free style program, she pulled up to second place overall in the rankings. Dorothy was right behind Dianne deLeeuw of The Netherlands who won the gold medal.

As she stood with Dianne and bronze medalist, Christine

Winners of the 1975 World's Figure Skating Championship in Colorado Springs, Colo. L to R: Dorothy (2nd); Dianne deLeeuw (1st) skating for The Netherlands; Christine Errath (3rd), East Germany. (Courtesy Broadmoor Hotel.)

Errath, on the winner's platform, Dorothy knew they were all thinking ahead to the competition next year. The three girls had been training and competing for many years now and all their efforts were leading up to the 1976 Olympics. Who would win the coveted gold medal? Even the experts couldn't agree. They would only say that any one of the three girls could win.

In November Dorothy flew back to New York for another appearance in Superskates II. Again this program would benefit the Olympic fund. Dorothy enjoyed these exhibitions because she got to see her skating friends who also appeared in the shows. Sometimes they clowned around before a performance. Once Dorothy put on an oversized jacket that fell to her knees and walked around in it like an old-time comic. Another time she skated with short, choppy steps like a beginner during her warm-up time. After her performance Dorothy pretended that she didn't want to return to the ice and allowed herself to be pushed on by a tall, handsome young friend.

Dorothy was interviewed by reporters often now. She described the full schedule she followed to stay in condition. Were the sacrifices worth it, she was asked.

"Being in the Olympics will make it all worthwhile," she replied.

Before an appearance in a New Jersey skating show, Dorothy found time to have a photo session with her old friend, David Leonardi. It was a beautiful fall afternoon. Autumn leaves fell all around them as David snapped one color picture after another. Then one leaf came to rest on Dorothy's head as she stood under a tree in her friend's back yard. Just for an instant, it seemed to resemble a small crown. Could it possibly be an omen of things to come at the Olympics?

(Below, right) Clowning around during practice for the Olympic Tribute Show at Wilmington, Delaware. Dorothy with Kent Weigle, a member of the 1976 Olympic and World Gold Dance Team.

Chapter Eight

Dorothy won her third National Senior ladies title at the Broadmoor in January, but her thoughts already were on Innsbruck. There was so much to be done before the Olympics began in that Austrian town on February 4th.

First Dorothy flew to Toronto and worked on free style with choreographer Brian Foley. Together they set each element of her program to the music she had chosen. Then back in Connecticut, Dorothy's father put the selections of music on one tape so that the fast and slow tempos were perfectly timed to the skating program. In New York Dorothy visited the boot and skate shop and then went to the dressmaker for final fittings.

And now it was time to go. Her sister, Marcia, hugged and kissed her at the front door. "Good luck," she whispered.

Pinch me somebody, Dorothy thought. I'm actually on my way to the Olympics.

With her mother Dorothy left for Innsbruck ahead of the rest of the family. She still needed more training with Carlo. Her father, sister, brother, and sister-in-law would come later. Finally for the first time since Sandy's wedding, the entire family would be together for more than just a few hours. Just as Dorothy's skating had separated the family, it was now bringing them together again at Innsbruck.

Dorothy executing her compulsory school figures at the 1976 Nationals in Colorado Springs. The judges observe at close range during these intricate tracings. Shown on Dorothy's jacket are the seven skating pins awarded for the seven tests passed. (The eighth award is a small gold medal.)

Scenes from Dorothy's 2-minute compulsory program at the 1976 Nationals.

On February 4, the 1976 Winter Olympics officially began. In colorful ceremonies in the huge outdoor stadium, banners flew in the wind as the Olympic torch was set aflame. Dressed in red jackets, blue slacks, and white stocking hats, the United States team drew a tremendous roar from the crowd when they marched in. Dorothy felt proud and excited and honored to be a part of all the pageantry.

The pressure began to build as Dorothy waited for the Figure Skating competition to begin. She'd heard it said that she was inconsistent at times because of her stage fright. That had been true. And she had heard comments criticizing her for leaving out several jumps in her program last month at Nationals. She knew she couldn't do that now at Innsbruck. The competition was too close and too

tough. "I owe so much to so many wonderful people that I'm determined to overcome anything for the Olympics," Dorothy told herself.

Compulsory school figures were the first to be skated. When all the scores were tallied, Dorothy placed second. She had skated unusually well in the figures. Everyone began to say that she would win the gold medal. They all wanted to talk to her. The pressures mounted. To help her concentrate totally on her performance, the team officials secluded Dorothy from the public.

On Wednesday while practicing for the short program, Dorothy fell during a sit spin. She had always been frightened of falling during a performance. Now she had fallen during a practice and that seemed to take some of the pressure away from her for the moment. She went out and

skated a nearly perfect short program and took over the lead.

And finally it was Friday, the 13th. If Dorothy was superstitious, she didn't show it. She put on a red skating dress, trimmed with white at the neck and cuffs. She fastened her gold four-leaf clover pin on her shoulder and selected a favorite pair of earrings. Then she brushed her short, dark hair, applied some lipstick and she was ready.

Dorothy said goodbye to her mother, who stayed at the hotel because she was too nervous to watch the competition. Then, with her father, Dorothy went to the stadium and waited. Up in the stands she saw a sign that read: "Which of the West: Dorothy." What did it mean? Which skater from the West—Dorothy? Or, World champion Dianne de Leeuw? Under the printed letters there was a rainbow. Dorothy's fans were comparing her to Dorothy in the *Wizard of Oz* and wishing her well on her own journey down the yellow-brick-road to the gold medal. She burst into tears and cried on her father's shoulder. Then she felt better as some of the pressure eased, and she smiled.

One by one the skaters presented their programs. Finally, in the fourteenth spot, it was Dorothy's turn. She skated to the center of the rink and felt totally alone now in the midst of all those people. As the opening strains of music from *The Seahawk* began, Dorothy's smile flooded the stadium. Quickly she stroked into her first move and her delayed Axel brought immediate applause. Feeling the audience with her, clapping as she moved through the four

Wearing a different costume, Dorothy glides through her 4-minute program at the Nationals.

minutes, she sometimes felt like she was floating. Other times she felt nothing at all. She swept through the Walleys, a high, clean double Lutz, a butterfly and a lay-back spin, split jumps and then into her famous Hamill camel. Skimming lightly over the ice, Dorothy skated totally with her music, feeling every note as she moved through the fast, strong program. Then, with a final scratch spin, it was over.

The audience cheered and clapped. They threw so many flowers on the ice that four other skaters had to help Dorothy pick them up. Finally she skated off and hugged Carlo and her father and then waited for her marks. She smiled happily when she saw the scores. Nearly all of them were 5.8's for technical ability and 5.9's for artistic merit.

(Top, left) On her way to the podium. (Bottom, left) 1976 Nationals winners, Linda Fratianne (2nd), Dorothy (1st), and Wendy Burge (3rd). (Top, right) Dorothy holding the Owen Memorial Trophy as the 1976 Nationals champion. (Below) Innsbruck, Austria, scene of the 1976 Olympic Winter Games. (Courtesy Austrian National Tourist Office.)

After everyone had skated, the announcer presented the winners.

"In third place, Christine Errath of East Germany. In second place, Dianne de Leeuw of The Netherlands. And in first place, Dorothy Hamill of the United States."

Dorothy stepped to the winners' platform to stand between Christine and Dianne. The magic moment had arrived. An official placed a red and white ribbon around her neck. On it hung the beautiful gold medal which she'd dreamed about for so many years. Her smile warmed the far corners of the huge stadium as she waved to the cheering audience and clamoring photographers. Then, as the orchestra played *The Star Spangled Banner*, Dorothy fought to control her overwhelming emotions. She had never been happier than at that moment. She was Dorothy Hamill, Olympic Champion.

A dream come true. Dorothy proudly shows the gold medal she was awarded at the 12th Winter Olympic Games. (Courtesy Wide World Photos.)

Epilogue

Several weeks later, in Goteborg, Sweden, Dorothy won the World competition first place gold medal also. She joined three other American women skaters, Tenley Albright, Carol Heiss, and Peggy Fleming, in making a clean sweep of all the national and international figure skating titles.

After the official ceremonies were over, Dick Button interviewed Dorothy on television.

"What are you going to do now, Dorothy?" he asked.

"I'm going to smoke a cigar," she said, smiling impishly into the camera.

"What's next for you, Dorothy?" Dick asked.

"I'm going on tour for a month," she replied. "Then I hope to have a few weeks of rest before I make up my mind what I'll do. Right now I'm on Cloud Nine."

Then, as if he might be speaking for all her friends everywhere, Dick Button said, "Thank you for being a champion skater and a champion young lady."

About the Author

Elizabeth Van Steenwyk has written for magazines, TV, and radio. A graduate of Knox College in Galesburg, Illinois, her hometown, Mrs. Van Steenwyk now makes her home with her husband and their four children in San Marino, California. *Dorothy Hamill: Olympic Champion* is her first book for Harvey House. It will be followed this fall by another title in the *Women in Sports Series*. An avid sports fan herself, Mrs. Van Steenwyk and her husband enjoy back-packing as well as watching their children compete in school athletics.

About the Photographer

David Leonardi, who specializes in ice skating photography on week-ends and vacations, is a graphic designer in Philadelphia. He first saw Dorothy Hamill skate in 1968 while in Lake Placid, New York, on a ski trip. Mr. Leonardi grew up in Camden, New Jersey, and graduated from the Philadelphia Museum School of Industrial Arts (now Philadelphia College of Art). He served in the China-Burma-India Theatre with the U.S. Air Force during World War II. He makes his home in Collingswood, New Jersey.